Little Science Stories

The Sun Is Hot

By Amanda Geb

The Sun keeps Earth warm.

It can make things hot.

 It can make our skin hot.

It can make sand hot.

 It can make black top hot.

It can make it too hot to play.

Feel grass in the bright sun.

Feel grass in the shade.

Is it warmer in the sun?

Feel sand in the bright sun.

 Feel sand in the shade.

Is it cooler in the shade?

Word List

science words

cooler	Sun
Earth	sun
hot	warm

sight words

cooler	the
Earth	to
our	warm
The	warmer

Vowel Teams

/ā/ay	/ē/ee	/ī/igh	/o͞o/oo
play	Feel	bright	too
	keeps		

Try It!

Get two tubs of sand. Place a tub of sand in the sun.
Place the other in the shade. Wait an hour.
Which sand is warmer?

69 Words

The Sun keeps Earth warm.

It can make things hot.

It can make our skin hot.

It can make sand hot.

It can make black top hot.

It can make it too hot to play.

Feel grass in the bright sun.

Feel grass in the shade.

Is it warmer in the sun?

Feel sand in the bright sun.

Feel sand in the shade.

Is it cooler in the shade?

CHERRY BLOSSOM PRESS

Published in the United States of America by Cherry Lake Publishing Group
Ann Arbor, Michigan
www.cherrylakepublishing.com

Photo Credits: © XiXinXing/Shutterstock, cover, title page; © Chesterf/Dreamstime.com, 2; © Piyaset/Shutterstock, 3; © Ground Picture/Shutterstock, 4; © Crazy80frog/Dreamstime.com, 5; © canadastock/Shutterstock, 6; © Slaohome/Shutterstock, 7; © Studio 1One/Shutterstock, 8; © TinnaPong/Shutterstock, 9; © Serg64/Shutterstock, 10; © Zurijeta/Shutterstock, 11; © Polo Jimenez/Dreamstime.com, 12; © Vitalii Bashkatov/Shutterstock, 13; © Chiangmaisabaaidee/ Shutterstock, back cover

Cherry Blossom Press is an imprint of Cherry Lake Publishing Group.

Library of Congress Cataloging-in-Publication Data

Names: Gebhardt, Amanda, author.
Title: The sun is hot / written by Amanda Gebhardt.
Description: Ann Arbor, Michigan : Cherry Blossom Press, [2024] | Series:
  Little science stories | Audience: Grades K-1 | Summary: "Investigate
  how the Sun warms Earth in this decodable science book for beginning
  readers. A combination of domain-specific sight words and sequenced
  phonics skills builds confidence in content area reading. Bold, colorful
  photographs align directly with the text to help readers strengthen
  comprehension"— Provided by publisher.
Identifiers: LCCN 2023035056 | ISBN 9781668937709 (paperback) | ISBN
  9781668940082 (ebook) | ISBN 9781668941430 (pdf)
Subjects: LCSH: Sun—Juvenile literature. | Earth (Planet)—Juvenile
  literature.
Classification: LCC QB521.5 .G43 2023 | DDC 523.7–dc23/eng/20230824
LC record available at https://lccn.loc.gov/2023035056

Printed in the United States of America

Amanda Gebhardt is a curriculum writer and editor and a life-long learner. She lives in Ann Arbor, Michigan, with her husband, two kids, and one playful pup named Cookie.